Śrī Lalitā Triśatī Stotra

Mata Amritanandamayi Center
San Ramon, California, United States

Śrī Lalitā Triśatī Stotra

Published by:
Mata Amritanandamayi Center
P.O. Box 613
San Ramon, CA 94583
United States

First Edition: September 2015

In India:
www.amritapuri.org
inform@amritapuri.org

In USA:
www.amma.org

In Europe:
www.amma-europe.org

Contents

Introduction	4
Dhyānam	6
Śrī Lalitā Triśatī Stotra	10
Closing Prayers	51
Guru Stotram	53
Devī Bhujaṅgam	58
Annapūrṇa Stotram	66
Bhagavad Gītā – Chapter 8	75
Amma's Websites	87

Introduction

The Three Hundred Names of the Divine Mother

The Śrī Lalitā Triśatī Stotra or Śrī Lalitā Triśatī Stotram is part of the Lalitopakhyanam chapter of the Brahmanda Purana. It is a hymn in praise of the female aspect of the Divine. Śrī Lalitā Triśatī is a highly revered Sanskrit stotra, which contains the 300 Divine Names of Goddess Lalitā or the Divine Mother. Similar to the Śrī Lalitā Sahasranāmam, the Śrī Lalitā Triśatī Stotra is a conversation between Sage Agasthya and Lord Hayagrīva (the avatar of Lord Vishnu with a horse head).

The Śrī Lalitā Triśatī Stotra is considered to be the most secret of the stotras. The name Lalitā means "She Who Plays", and play (līla) refers to the creation and sustaining of the universe. Creation, manifestation and dissolution are all considered a play of Devi. She is the transcendent beauty of the three worlds.

Dhyānam

Meditation

sindūrāruṇa–vigrahāṁ tri–nayanām
māṇikya–mauli–sphurat–tārā
nāyaka–śekharām smitamukhīm
āpīna–vakṣoruhām
pāṇibhyām alipūrṇa–ratna–caṣakam
raktotpalam–bibhratīm
saumyāṁ ratna–ghaṭastha–rakta–
caraṇāṁ dhyāyet parām ambikām

O Mother Ambika, I meditate on Your resplendent red form with three sacred eyes, wearing a sparkling crown jewel and the crescent moon and displaying a sweet smile, with Your large breasts brimming with motherly love holding in each hand jewel-studded vessels decked with red lotus flowers which are encircled by bees, and with Your red lotus feet resting on a golden jar filled with jewels!

dhyāyet padmāsanasthām vikasita–
vadanām padma–patrāyatākṣīm
hemābhām pītavastrām kara–kalita–
lasad–hema–padmām varāṅgim
sarvālaṅkāra–yuktām satatam
abhayadām bhaktanamrām
bhavānīm
śrī-vidyām śānta-mūrtīm sakala–sura–
nutāṁ sarva–sampat–pradātrīm

O Mother, let me meditate on Your beautiful form with the color of gold, with a beaming face and large lotus eyes, sitting in the lotus flower wearing a yellow garment and resplendent with all ornaments, holding a golden lotus in Your hand, worshipped by the bowing devotees and always giving refuge! Let me meditate on You, O Śrī Vidya, embodiment of peace, the object of worship by all the devas, and the bestower of all the riches!

sakuṅkuma–vilepanām alika–cumbi–
kastūrikām
samanda–hasitekṣaṇām saśara–cāpa
pāśāṅkuśām
aśeṣa–jana–mohinīm aruṇa–mālya-
bhūṣojvalām
japā–kusuma–bhāsurām japa-vidhau
smared ambikām

O Mother of the Universe, as I sit for japa, let me remember Your form with the beauty of the hibiscus flower, wearing a red garland and sparkling ornaments, smeared with red saffron, shinning with a mark of musk on your forehead whose fragrance is attracting the bees, holding in your hands the bow and the arrow, the noose and the goad, and displaying a gen-tle smile, throwing sweet glances, and beguiling everyone!

aruṇāṁ karuṇā–taraṅgitākṣīṁ
dhṛta–pāśāṅkuśa puṣpa–bāṇa–cāpām
aṇimādibhir āvṛtām mayūkhair
aham ityeva vibhāvaye maheśīm

O Great Goddess, let me imagine that I am one with Your glorious red form, surrounded by the golden rays from Anima and the other eight divine glories, holding the noose and the goad, the bow and the arrows of flowers, with eyes in which rise waves of compassion!

Śrī Lalitā Triśatī Stotra

1. **Om kakāra rūpāyai namaḥ**
   She who is the letter 'ka'-this letter represents light. This is the first letter of the 'pañcadasākṣari' mantra (15 syllable mantra).
2. **Om kalyāṇyai namaḥ**
   She who is auspicious.
3. **Om kalyāṇa guṇa śāliṇyai namaḥ**
   She who is the personification of good qualities.
4. **Om kalyāṇa śaila nilayāyai namaḥ**
   She who resides in the auspicious mountain (Himalaya).
5. **Om kamanīyāyai namaḥ**
   She who is desirable.
6. **Om kalāvatyai namaḥ**
   She who possesses all arts.
7. **Om kamalākṣyai namaḥ**
   She who has lotus-like eyes.

8. Om kanmaṣa ghnyai namaḥ
She who destroys impurities.

9. Om karuṇāmṛta sāgarāyai namaḥ
She who is the Ocean of the nectar of compassion.

10. Om kadamba kānanā vāsāyai namaḥ
She who lives in the forest of Kadamba trees (a blue flowering tree).

11. Om kadamba kusuma priyāyai namaḥ
She who likes the flowers of the Kadamba tree.

12. Om kandarpa vidyāyai namaḥ
She who is the knowledge used by Cupid.

13. Om kandarpa janakāpāṅga vīkṣaṇāyai namaḥ
She who created Cupid by her glance alone.

14. Om karpūra vīṭi saurabhya kallolita kakuptaṭāyai namaḥ

She whose mouth is fragrant from chewing on the betel leaf, mixed with camphor and other ingredients.

15. Om kali doṣa harāyai namaḥ
She who destroys the bad effects of Kali yuga.

16. Om kañja locanāyai namaḥ
She who has eyes like a lotus.

17. Om kamra vigrahāyai namaḥ
She who has a desirable form.

18. Om karmādi sākṣiṇyai namaḥ
She who is the witness of actions, thought and words.

19. Om kārayitryaī namaḥ
She who controls all actions.

20. Om karma phala pradāyai namaḥ
She who gives the fruit of one's actions.

21. Om ekāra rūpāyai namaḥ
She who is the letter 'e'. 'E' denotes the absolute truth, Brahman. This is the second letter of the 'pañcadasākṣari' mantra.

22. Om ekākṣaryai namaḥ
She who is the single syllable ('Om').

23. Om ekānekākṣarā kṛtāyai namaḥ
She who manifests the single syllable 'Om', and all other letters as well.

24. Om etat taditya nirdeśyāyai namaḥ
She who cannot be indicated as 'this' or 'that'.

25. Om ekānanda cidākṛtayai namaḥ
She who is the form of non-dual bliss and consciousness.

26. Om evam ityāgamābodhyāyai namaḥ
She whom the Vedas cannot describe.

27. Om eka bhaktimad arcitāyai namaḥ
She who is worshipped by those with one-pointed devotion.

28. Om ekāgra citta nirdhyātāyai namaḥ
She who can be meditated on by a one-pointed mind.

29. Om eṣaṇā rahitā dṛtāyai namaḥ
She who is the refuge of those without worldly desires.

30. Om elā sugandhi cikurāyai namaḥ
She whose hair has the sweet smell of cardamom.

31. Om enaḥ kūṭa vināśinyai namaḥ
She who destroys bundles of impurities.

32. Om eka bhogāyai namaḥ
She who has only one experience (Self-experience).

33. Om eka rasāyai namaḥ
She who has only Bliss (Bliss of the Self).

34. Om ekaiśvarya pradāyinyai namaḥ
She who gives the glory of Oneness.

35. Om ekātapatra sāmrājya pradāyai namaḥ
She who gives you the power of the emperor of the world.

36. Om ekānta pūjitāyai namaḥ

She who is worshipped with a one-pointed mind.

37. Om edhamāna prabhāyai namaḥ
She who has the foremost luster.

38. Om ekad aneka jagadīśvaryai namaḥ
She who is the Ruler of the universe of Oneness and duality.

39. Om eka vīrādi samsevyāyai namaḥ
She who is worshipped by valorous warriors.

40. Om eka prābhava śālinyai namaḥ
She who has the power of the One Truth.

41. Om īkāra rūpāyai namaḥ
She who is the letter 'ī'. 'Ī' denotes Shakti. This is the third letter of the 'pañcadasākṣari' mantra.

42. Om īśitryai namaḥ
She who rules everything.

43. Om īpsitārtha pradāyinyai namaḥ
She who gives the objects one desires.

44. Om īdṛgityavinird eśyāyai namaḥ
She who cannot be indicated by attributes.

45. Om īśvaratva vidhāyinyai namaḥ
She who makes Brahman into the Creator, Sustainer and Destroyer.

46. Om īśānādi brahma mayyai namaḥ
She who is in the form of the five gods, viz Brahma, Vishnu, Rudra, Īsha, and Sadāshiva.

47. Om īśitvādyaṣṭa siddhidāyai namaḥ
She who gives the eight super-natural powers.

48. Om īkṣitryai namaḥ
She who sees all.

49. Om īkṣaṇa sṛṣṭāṇḍa koṭyai namaḥ
She who creates millions of galaxies by a mere glance.

50. Om īśvara vallabhāyai namaḥ
She who is the beloved of Shiva.

51. Om īḍitāyai namaḥ
She who is praised in the holy books like Vedas, Puranas, etc.

52. Om īśvarārdhāṅga śarīrāyai namaḥ
She whose body is half Shiva.

53. Om īśādhi devatāyai namaḥ
She who is deity supreme even to Shiva.

54. Om īśvara preraṇa karyai namaḥ
She who prompts the actions of Shiva (Creation, etc.).

55. Om īśa tāṇḍava sākṣiṇyai namaḥ
She who is the witness of the cosmic dance of Shiva.

56. Om īśvarotsaṅga nilayāyai namaḥ
She who abides in union with Shiva.

57. Om īti bādhā vināśinyai namaḥ
She who destroys unexpected calamities.

58. Om īhā virahitāyai namaḥ
She who is devoid of desire.

59. Om īśa śaktyai namaḥ
She who is the power of Shiva.

60. Om īṣat smitānanāyai namaḥ
She who has a soft smile on Her face.

61. Om lakāra rūpāyai namaḥ
She who is the letter 'la'. 'La' denotes the wave which initiates wisdom. This is the fourth letter of the 'pañcadasākṣari' mantra.

62. Om lalitāyai namaḥ
She who is known by the name of 'Lalitā' (One who abides in simplicity).

63. Om lakṣmī vāṇī niṣevitāyai namaḥ
She who is attended on by Lakshmi (the goddess of wealth) and Saraswati (the goddess of knowledge).

64. Om lākinyai namaḥ
She who is easily approachable.

65. Om lalanā rūpāyai namaḥ
She who can be seen as the goddess in all women.

66. Om lasad dāḍima pāṭalāyai namaḥ
She whose skin is the color of a blossomed pomegranate flower.

67. Om lasantikā lasat phālāyai namaḥ
She who has a shining forehead with the beautiful *tilaka* (dot).

68. Om lalāṭa nayanārcitāyai namaḥ
She who is worshipped by yogis whose eyes of wisdom are awa-kened.

69. Om lakṣaṇojjvala divyāṅgyai namaḥ
She whose limbs have all auspicious qualities.

70. Om lakṣa koṭyaṇḍa nāyikāyai namaḥ
She who rules billions of galaxies.

71. Om lakṣyārthāyai namaḥ
She who is the inner experience behind all the Vedic proclamations.

72. Om lakṣaṇāgamyāyai namaḥ
She who cannot be understood by characteristics.

73. Om labdhakāmāyai namaḥ
She whose desires are fulfilled.

74. Om latātanave namah
She whose body resembles a fine creeper.

75. Om lalāmarā jadalikāyai namaḥ
She who has a *tilaka* made of musk on the forehead.

76. Om lambi muktā latāñcitāyai namaḥ
She who is decorated with a hanging pearl heelball.

77. Om lambodara prasave namaḥ
She who is the mother of Ganesha.

78. Om labhyāyai namaḥ
She who is attainable.

79. Om lajjāḍhyāyai namaḥ
She who has the quality of shyness.

80. Omlaya varjitāyai namaḥ
She who is never destroyed.

81. Om hrīmkāra rūpāyai namaḥ
She who is the sacred syllable 'hrīm'- the fifth letter of the 'pañcadasākṣari' mantra.

82. Om hrīmkāra nilayāyai namaḥ
She who abides in the sacred syllable 'hrīm'.

83. Om hrīm pada priyāyai namaḥ
She who is fond of the mantra 'hrīm'.

84. Om hrīmkāra bījāyai namaḥ
She who is the seed of the sound 'hrīm'.

85. Om hrīmkāra mantrāyai namaḥ
She whose mantra is the sound 'hrīm'.

86. Om hrīmkāra lakṣaṇāyai namaḥ
She who is indicated by the sound 'hrīm'.

87. Om hrīmkāra japa suprītāyai namaḥ
She who is very pleased by japa of 'hrīm'.

88. Om hrīmatyai namaḥ
She who is endowed with modesty.

89. Om hrīm vibhūṣaṇāyai namaḥ
She whose ornament is the sound 'hrīm'.

90. Om hrīm śīlāyai namaḥ
She who manifests 'hrīm'.

91. Om hrīm padārādhyāyai namaḥ
She who is worshipped by the sound 'hrīm'.

92. Om hrīm garbhāyai namaḥ
She who is the source of 'hrīm'.

93. Om hrīm padābidhāyai namaḥ
She who is known by the sound 'hrīm'.

94. Om hrīmkāra vācyāyai namaḥ
She who is indicated by 'hrīm'.

95. Om hrīmkāra pūjyāyai namaḥ
She who is to be worshipped by 'hrīm'.

96. Om hrīmkāra pīṭhikāyai namaḥ
She who is the basis of 'hrīm'.

97. Om hrīmkāra vedyāyai namaḥ
She who is known by 'hrīm'.

98. Om hrīmkāra cintyāyai namaḥ
She who can be thought of through 'hrīm'.

99. Om hrīm namaḥ
She who is 'hrīm'.

100. Om hrīm śarīriṇyai namaḥ
She whose body is 'hrīm'.

101. Om hakāra rūpāyai namaḥ
She who is of the letter 'ha'. This letter indicates the valour which kills enemies. This is the sixth letter of the 'pañcadasākṣari' mantra.

102. Om hala dhṛt pūjitāyai namaḥ

She who is worshipped by Balarāma (elder brother of Sri Krishna).

103. Om hariṇekṣaṇāyai namaḥ

She whose eyes are like a deer's.

104. Om hara priyāyai namaḥ

She who is the beloved of Shiva.

105. Om harārādhyāyai namaḥ

She who is worshipped by Shiva.

106. Om hari brahmendra vanditāyai namaḥ

She who is worshipped by Vishnu, Brahma and Indra.

107. Om hayā rūḍhā sevitāṅghryai namaḥ

She who is worshiped by the horse mounted cavalry.

108. Om hayamedha samarcitāyai namaḥ

She who is worshipped by the Aswamedha sacrifice.

109. Om haryakṣa vāhanāyai namaḥ
She who rides the lion (Durga).

110. Om hamsa vāhanāyai namaḥ
She who rides the swan (Saraswati).

111. Om hata dānavāyai namaḥ
She by whom the demons were killed.

112. Om hatyādi pāpa śamanyai namaḥ
She who destroys even grave sins such as killing.

113. Om harid aśvādi sevitāyai namaḥ
She who is worshipped by him who rides the green horse (Indra).

114. Om hasti kumbhottuṅga kucāyai namaḥ
She who has breasts as upright as the forehead of the elephant.

115. Om hasti kṛtti priyāṅganāyai namaḥ
She who is the darling of him who wears elephant skin (Shiva).

116. Om haridrā kumkumā digdhāyai namaḥ

She whose body is scented with turmeric powder and *kumkum* (saffron).

117. Om haryaśvādya marārcitāyai namaḥ

She who is worshipped by devas such as Indra.

118. Om harikeśa sakhyai namaḥ

She who is the friend of Shiva.

119. Om hādi vidyāyai namaḥ

She who is the science of the 'pañca-dasākṣari' mantra.

120. Om hālā madollāsāyai namaḥ

She who is drunk with wine which was created from the ocean of milk.

121. Om sakāra rūpāyai namaḥ

She who is the letter 'sa' – which denotes material wealth and pleasures. 'Sa' is the sixth letter of the 'pañcadasākṣari' mantra.

122. Om sarvajñāyai namaḥ

She who is omniscient.

123. Om sarveśyai namaḥ
She who rules over all.

124. Om sarva maṅgalāyai namaḥ
She who is all auspiciousness.

125. Om sarva kartryai namaḥ
She who is the doer of all actions.

126. Om sarva bhartryai namaḥ
She who protects eveything.

127. Om sarva hantryai namaḥ
She who destroys everything.

128. Om sanātanāyai namaḥ
She who is eternal.

129. Om sarvānavadyāyai namaḥ
She who has no fault at all.

130. Om sarvāṅga sundaryai namaḥ
She whose entire form is beautiful.

131. Om sarva sākṣiṇyai namaḥ
She who is the witness of everything.

132. Om sarvātmikāyai namaḥ
She who is the essence of everything.

133. Om sarva saukhya dātryai namaḥ

She who gives all happiness.

134. Om sarva vimohinyai namaḥ
She who deludes all.

135. Om sarvādhārāyai namaḥ
She who is the substratum of everything.

136. Om sarva gatāyai namaḥ
She who is all pervading.

137. Om sarva viguṇa varjitāyai namaḥ
She who is devoid of defects.

138. Om sarvāruṇāyai namaḥ
She whose body is slightly reddish.

139. Om sarva mātre namaḥ
She who is the mother of all.

140. Om sarva bhūṣaṇa bhūṣitāyai namaḥ
She who is decorated with all ornaments.

141. Om kakārārthāyai namaḥ
She who is the meaning of the letter 'ka' - This letter 'ka' represents light. This is the eighth letter of the 'pañcadasākṣari' mantra.

142. Om kāla hantryai namaḥ
She who is the destroyer of death.

143. Om kāmeṣyai namaḥ
She who controls all desires.

144. Om kāmitārthadāyai namaḥ
She who grants the objects of desire.

145. Om kāma sañjīvanyai namaḥ
She who brought the god of love back to life.

146. Om kalyāyai namaḥ
She who is capable of creation.

147. Om kaṭhina stana maṇḍalāyai namaḥ
She who has firm breasts.

148. Om kara bhorave namaḥ
She who has thighs like the elephant's trunk.

149. Om kalā nāthā mukhyai namaḥ
She whose face is like the full moon.

150. Om kaca jitāmbudāyai namaḥ

She who has hair which resembles the dark cloud.

151. Om kaṭākṣa syandi karuṇāyai namaḥ
She whose glance is full of compassion.

152. Om kapāli prāṇa nāyikāyai namaḥ
She who is the wife of Lord Shiva.

153. Om kāruṇya vigrahāyai namaḥ
She who is the personification of compassion.

154. Om kāntāyai namaḥ
She who is beautiful.

155. Om kānti bhūta japāvalyai namaḥ
She whose luster is like the hibiscus flower.

156. Om kalālāpāyai namaḥ
She who engages in the arts.

157. Om kambu kaṇṭhyai namaḥ
She whose neck has folds like a spiral shell.

158. Om kara nirjita pallavāyai namaḥ
She whose hands are softer than tender leaf buds.

159. Om kalpa vallī sama bhujāyai namaḥ
She whose arms are like wish-fulfilling creepers.

160. Om kastūri tilakāñcitāyai namaḥ
She who wears a dot of musk in between the eyebrows.

161. Om hakārārthāyai namaḥ
She who is the meaning of the letter 'ha'. This letter 'ha' represents money, valour etc. This is the ninth letter of the 'pañcadasākṣari' mantra.

162. Om hamsa gatyai namaḥ
She who moves like a swan.

163. Om hāṭakābharaṇojjvalāyai namaḥ
She who shines wearing gold ornaments.

164. Om hāra hāri kucā bhogāyai namaḥ
She whose breasts are decorated by beautiful garlands.

165. Om hākinyai namaḥ
She who cuts the bondages.

166. Om halya varjitāyai namaḥ

She who is devoid of bad qualities.

167. Om haritpati samārādhyāyai namaḥ

She who is being worshipped by those eight gods who guard the different directions *(dig palakas)*.

168. Om haṭhātkāra hatāsurāyai namaḥ

She who killed *asuras* quickly by her valour.

169. Om harṣa pradāyai namaḥ

She who gives happiness.

170. Om havir bhoktryai namaḥ

She who partakes the offering given to sacrifice in fire.

171. Om hārda santamas āpahāyai namaḥ

She who removes darkness from the heart.

172. Om hallīsa lāsya santuṣṭāyai namaḥ

She who is pleased with *rasa lila*.

173. Om hamsa mantrārtha rūpiṇyai namaḥ

She who is the meaning of the '*hamsa*' mantra ('*So ham*', 'I am He').

174. Om hānopādāna vinirmuktāyai namaḥ

She who is free from loss and gain.

175. Om harṣiṇyai namaḥ

She who is delighted.

176. Om hari sodaryai namaḥ

She who is the sister of Lord Vishnu.

177. Om hāhā hūhū mukha stutyāyai namaḥ

She who is being praised by celestial beings called Hāhā and Hūhū.

178. Om hāni vṛddhi vivārjitāyai namaḥ

She who is beyond destruction and growth.

179. Om hayyaṅgavīna hṛdayāyai namaḥ

She who has a heart that melts like butter.

180. Om harigopāruṇāmśukāyai namaḥ

She who is of red colour.

181. Om lakārākhyāyai namaḥ

She whose is the letter 'la'. This is the tenth letter of the 'pañcadasākṣari' mantra.

182. Om latā pūjyāyai namaḥ

She who is being worshipped by chaste women.

183. Om laya sthityut bhav eśvaryai namaḥ

She who is the controller of dissolution, sustainment and manifestation.

184. Om lāsya darśana santuṣṭāyai namaḥ

She who becomes pleased by seeing dance.

185. Om lābhālābha vivarjitāyai namaḥ

She who has neither gain nor loss.

186. Om laṅghyetarājñāyai namaḥ

She who does not obey others' orders.

187. Om lāvaṇya śalinyai namaḥ

She who is of unmatched beauty.

188. Om laghu siddhidāyai namaḥ

She who gives attainments easily.

189. Om lākṣā rasa savarṇābhāyai namaḥ

She who shines like the color of *lākṣā*-juice (a bright violet plant).

190. Om lakṣmaṇāgraja pūjitāyai namaḥ

She who was worshipped by Lord Rama (elder brother of Lakshmana).

191. Om labhyetarāyai namaḥ

She who is attainable by others.

192. Om labdha bhakti sulabhāyai namaḥ

She who can be easily attained by devotion (*bhakti*).

193. Om lāṅgalāyudhāyai namaḥ

She who has a plough as a weapon (in her form of Adisesha).

194. Om lagna cāmara hasta śrī śāradā parivījitāyai namaḥ

She who is served by Lakshmi and Saraswati.

195. Om lajjāpada samārādhyāyai namaḥ

She who is worshipped by those who are modest.

196. Om lampaṭāyai namaḥ

She who has hidden herself from the earthly principles.

197. Om lakuleśvaryai namaḥ

She in whom the communities in the world merge.

198. Om labdha mānāyai namaḥ

She who is praised by all.

199. Om labdha rasāyai namaḥ

She who has attained the ultimate bliss.

200. Om labdha sampat samunnatyai namaḥ

She who has the apex of wealth.

201. Om hrīmkāriṇyai namaḥ

She who is the letter 'hrìm'. This is the eleventh letter of the 'pañcadasākṣari' mantra.

202. Om hrīmkārādyāyai namaḥ

She who is the origin of 'hrīm'.

203. Om hrīm madhyāyai namaḥ

She who is in the midst of 'hrīm'.

204. Om hrīm śikhāmaṇyai namaḥ

She who wears 'hrīm' in her head.

205. Om hrīmkāra kuṇḍāgni śikhāyai namaḥ

She who is the flame of the fire place (*homa kundam*) called 'hrīm'.

206. Om hrīmkāra śaśi candrikāyai namaḥ

She who is the nectar-like rays of the moon called 'hrīm'.

207. Om hrīmkāra bhāskara rucyai namaḥ

She who is the blissful rays of the sun called 'hrīm'.

208. Om hrīmkārāmboda cañcalāyai namaḥ

She who is the ray of lightning of the black clouds called 'hrīm'.

209. Om hrīmkāra kandāmkurikāyai namaḥ

She who is the germinating tendril of the tuber called 'hrīm'.

210. Om hrīmkāraika parāyaṇāyai namaḥ

She who completely relies on 'hrīm'.

211. Om hrīmkāra dīrghikā hamsyai namaḥ

She who is the swan playing in the canal called 'hrīm'.

212. Om hrīmkārodyāna kekinyai namaḥ

She who is the peahen playing in the garden of 'hrīm'.

213. Om hrīmkārāraṇya hariṇyai namaḥ
She who is the doe playing in the forest of 'hrīm'.

214. Om hrīmkārā lavā lavallyai namaḥ
She who is the ornamental climber in the flower bed of 'hrīm'.

215. Om hrīmkāra pañcara śukyai namaḥ
She who is the green parrot in the cage called 'hrīm'.

216. Om hrīmkārāṅgaṇa dīpikāyai namaḥ
She who is the light kept in the courtyard called 'hrīm'.

217. Om hrīmkāra kandarā simhyai namaḥ
She who is the lioness living in the cave called 'hrīm'.

218. Om hrīmkārāmbhoja bṛṅgikāyai namaḥ

She who is the insect playing in the lotus flower called 'hrīm'.

219. Om hrīmkāra sumano mādhvyai namaḥ

She who is the honey in the flower called 'hrīm'.

220. Om hrīmkāra taru mañjaryai namaḥ

She who is the flower bunch in the tree called 'hrīm'.

221. Om sakārākhyāyai namaḥ

She who is the letter 'sa', the twelfth letter of the 'pañcadasākṣari' mantra.

222. Om samarasāyai namaḥ

She who is evenly blissful in all situations.

223. Om sakalāgama samstutāyai namaḥ

She who is praised by all Vedas.

224. Om sarva vedānta tātparya bhūmyai namaḥ

She who is the place which is the essence of all Vedanta.

225. Om sad asad āśrayāyai namaḥ

She who is the foundation of what is and what is not.

226. Om sakalāyai namaḥ

She who is everything.

227. Om saccidānandāyai namaḥ

She who is Existence, Consciousness and Bliss.

228. Om sādhyāyai namaḥ

She who is to be attained.

229. Om sad gati dāyinyai namaḥ

She who gives salvation.

230. Om sanakādi muni dhyeyāyai namaḥ

She who is meditated on by sages like Sanaka.

231. Om sadā śiva kuṭumbinyai namaḥ

She who is the wife of Shiva.

232. Om sakalādhiṣṭhāna rūpāyai namaḥ
She who is the substratum of everything.

233. Om satya rūpāyai namaḥ
She who is the personification of truth.

234. Om samā kṛtayai namaḥ
She whose form is evenly shaped.

235. Om sarva prapañca nirmātryai namaḥ
She who constructs the entire universe.

236. Om samānādhika varjitāyai namaḥ
She who has neither equal nor superior.

237. Om sarvottuṅgāyai namaḥ
She who is the greatest among all.

238. Om saṅga hīnāyai namaḥ
She who has no attachments to anything.

239. Om saguṇāyai namaḥ
She who has good qualities.

240. Om sakaleṣṭadāyai namaḥ
She who fulfills all desires.

241. Om kakāriṇyai namaḥ
She who is the letter 'ka'. This is the thirteenth letter of the 'pañcadasākṣari' mantra.

242. Om kāvya lolāyai namaḥ
She who enjoys poetry.

243. Om kāmeśvara manoharāyai namaḥ
She who steals the mind of Shiva.

244. Om kāmeśvara prāṇa nāḍyai namaḥ
She who is the life-nerve of Shiva.

245. Om kāmeśotsaṅga vāsinyai namaḥ
She who sits on the left lap of Shiva.

246. Om kāmeśvarāliṅgitāṅgyai namaḥ
She who is embraced by Shiva.

247. Om kāmeśvara sukha pradāyai namaḥ
She who gives happiness to Shiva.

248. Om kāmeśvara praṇayinyai namaḥ
She who is the beloved of Shiva.

249. Om kāmeśvara vilāsinyai namaḥ
She who is the divine play of Shiva.

250. Om kāmeśvara tapaḥ siddhyai namaḥ
She who achieved Shiva through austerities.

251. Om kāmeśvara manaḥ priyāyai namaḥ
She who pleases the mind of Shiva.

252. Om kāmeśvara prāṇa nāthāyai namaḥ
She who is the life-controller of Shiva.

253. Om kāmeśvara vimohinyai namaḥ
She who deludes Shiva.

254. Om kāmeśvara brahma vidyāyai namaḥ
She who is the Absolute knowledge of Shiva.

255. Om kāmeśvara gṛheśvaryai namaḥ
She who is the lord of the house of Shiva.

256. Om kāmeśvarāhlāda karyai namaḥ
She who makes Shiva supremely happy.

257. Om kāmeśvara maheśvaryai namaḥ
She who is Shiva's Goddess.

258. Om kāmeśvaryai namaḥ
She who is Kameshwari, consort of Shiva.

259. Om kāma koṭi nilayāyai namaḥ
She who presides over the kāma kōṭi pīṭa in Kāñchīpuram.

260. Om kāṅkṣitārthadāyai namaḥ
She who fulfills the desires of devotees.

261. Om lakāriṇyai namaḥ
She who is the letter 'la'. This is the fourteenth letter of the 'pañcadasākṣari' mantra.

262. Om labdha rūpāyai namaḥ
She who has assumed a form.

263. Om labdha dhiyai namaḥ
She who is full of wisdom.

264. Om labdha vāñchitāyai namaḥ
She whose desires are all fulfilled.

265. Om labdha pāpa mano dūrāyai namaḥ

She who is far away from the reach of sinners.

266. Om labdhāhaṅkāra durgamāyai namaḥ

She who is difficult to attain by the egoistic.

267. Om labdha śaktyai namaḥ

She who has all powers.

268. Om labdha dehāyai namaḥ

She who assumes a body.

269. Om labdhaīśvarya samunnatyai namaḥ

She who has all glories.

270. Om labdha vṛddhyai namaḥ

She who has all prosperity.

271. Om labdha līlāyai namaḥ

She who enacts a play.

272. Om labdha yauvana śālinyai namaḥ

She who is ever young.

273. Om labdhātiśaya sarvāṅga saundaryāyai namaḥ
She who possesses astounding beauty of form.

274. Om labdha vibhramāyai namaḥ
She who enacts the play of maintaining the world.

275. Om labdha rāgāyai namaḥ
She who exists as love.

276. Om labdha pataye namaḥ
She who has Shiva as her husband.

277. Om labdha nānāgama sthityai namaḥ
She who manifests all Vedas.

278. Om labdha bhogāyai namaḥ
She who experiences all.

279. Om labdha sukhāyai namaḥ
She who enjoys happiness.

280. Om labdha harṣābhi pūritāyai namaḥ
She who is overfilled with delight.

281. Om hrīmkāra mūrtyai namaḥ

She who is the personification of the sound 'hrīm', the fifteenth and last letter of the 'pañcadasākṣari' mantra.

282. Om hrīmkāra saudha śṛiṅga kapotikāyai namaḥ

She who is the dove who lives in the top of the palace called 'hrīm'.

283. Om hrīmkāra dugdhābdhi sudhāyai namaḥ

She who is the nectar churned from the ocean of milk called 'hrīm'.

284. Om hrīmkāra kamalendirāyai namaḥ

She who is Goddess Lakshmi sitting on the lotus called 'hrīm'.

285. Om hrīmkāra maṇi dīparciṣe namaḥ

She who is the light of the ornamental lamp called 'hrīm'.

286. Om hrīmkāra taru śārikāyai namaḥ

She who is the lady bird sitting on the tree called 'hrīm'.

287. Om hrīmkāra peṭaka maṇyai namaḥ

She who is the pearl locked in the box called 'hrīm'.

288. Om hrīmkārādarśa bimbitāyai namaḥ

She who is the image reflected in the mirror called 'hrīm'.

289. Om hrīmkāra kośāsilatāyai namaḥ

She who is the shining sword in the sheath of 'hrīm'.

290. Om hrīmkārāsthāna nartakyai namaḥ

She who is the dancer on the stage called 'hrīm'.

291. Om hrīmkāra śuktikā muktāmaṇaye namaḥ

She who is the pearl found in the oyster shell called 'hrīm'.

292. Om hrīmkāra bodhitāyai namaḥ

She who is indicated by the sound 'hrīm'.

293. Om hrīmkāramaya sauvarṇa stambha vidruma putrikāyai namaḥ

She who is the coral statue on the shining pillars called 'hrīm'.

294. Om hrīmkāra vedopaniṣade namaḥ

She who is the Upanishad in the Veda called 'hrīm'.

295. Om hrīmkārā dhvara dakṣiṇāyai namaḥ

She who is the money gifted in the gate called 'hrīm'.

296. Om hrīmkāra nandanārāma nava kalpaka vallaryai namaḥ

She who is the new divine climber present in the garden called 'hrīm'.

297. Om hrīmkāra himavad gaṅgāyai namaḥ

She who is the river Ganga in the Himalaya mountain called 'hrīm'.

298. Om hrīmkārārṇava kaustubhāyai namaḥ

She who is the precious gem given birth by the ocean called 'hrīm'.

299. Om hrīmkāra mantra sarvasvāyai namaḥ

She who is the total wealth churned out of the mantra 'hrīm'.

300. Om hrīmkārapara saukhyadāyai namaḥ

She who gives the infinite happiness of 'hrīm'.

Closing Prayers

Om asatomā sadgamaya
tamasomā jyotirgamaya
mṛityormā amṛtamgamaya
om śāntiḥ śāntiḥ śāntiḥ

Om, lead us from untruth to Truth,
from darkness to light,
from death to immortality.
Om peace, peace, peace.

lokaḥ samastaḥ sukhino bhavantū
lokaḥ samastaḥ sukhino bhavantū
lokaḥ samastaḥ sukhino bhavantū

May all beings in all the worlds be happy.

oṁ śāntiḥ śāntiḥ śāntiḥ

Om peace, peace, peace.

oṁ śrī gurubhyo namaḥ harī oṁ

Om salutations to the guru.

Guru Stotram

Hymn to the Guru

Akhaṇḍamaṇḍalākaram/vyāptam yena carācaram
tatpadam darśitam yena/tasmai śrī gurave namaḥ /1

Salutations to the Guru who reveals the supreme, undivided essence that pervades this entire universe of moving and non-moving beings.

Ajñāna timirāndhasya/jñānāñjana śalākayā
cakṣurunmīlitam yena/tasmai śrī gurave namaḥ /2

Salutations to the Guru who rescues us from the darkness of ignorance and restores to us the vision of knowledge and of the Truth.

Gururbrahmā gururviṣṇuḥ/gururdevo maheśvaraḥ
guru sākṣāt param brahma/tasmai śrī gurave namaḥ /3

Salutations to the Guru who is Brahma, Visnu and Shiva. The Guru is the Supreme Brahman itself.

Sthāvaram jaṅgamam vyāptam/ yatkiñcit sacarācaram
tatpadam darśitam yena/tasmai śrī gurave namaḥ /4

Salutations to the Guru who reveals the essence of all beings, whether they be in motion or still, alive or dead.

Cinmayam vyāpiyat sarvam/trailokyam sacarācaram
tatpadam darśitam yena/tasmai śrī gurave namaḥ /5

Salutations to the Guru who reveals the pure intelligence that animates all of the moving and the non-moving beings in the three worlds.

Sarva śruti śiroratna/virājita padāmbujaḥ
vedāntāmbuja sūryo yaḥ/tasmai śrī gurave namaḥ /6

Salutations to the Guru whose blessed feet are adorned with the gems that are the revelations of the scriptures. The Guru is the sun that causes the flower of knowledge to bloom.

Caitanya śāśvata śānta/vyomātīto nirañjanaḥ
bindunādakalātītaḥ/tasmai śrī gurave namaḥ /7

Salutations to the Guru who is intelligence itself, who is the eternal, who dwells in everlasting peace and bliss beyond space and time, who is pure and who is beyond all sounds and vision.

Jñānaśakti samārūḍhaḥ/tattvamālā vibhūṣitaḥ
bhukti mukti pradātā ca/tasmai śrī gurave namaḥ /8

Salutations to the Guru who wields the power of knowledge, who is adorned with a garland of the gems of truth and who grants both material prosperity and spiritual liberation.

Anekajanma samprāpta/karmabandha vidāhine
ātma jñānā pradānena/tasmai śrī gurave namaḥ /9

Salutations to the Guru who reveals the light of knowledge and thus destroys the evil fate that has accumulated during countless births.

Śoṣaṇam bhavasindhośca/jñāpanam sārasampadaḥ
guroḥ pādodakam samyak/tasmai śrī gurave namaḥ /10

Salutations to the Guru, the water sanctified by the touch of whose feet dries up the ocean of illusion and reveals the true and only contentment.

Na guroradhikam tattvam/na guroradhikam tapaḥ

tattvajñānāt param nāsti/tasmai śrī gurave namaḥ /11

There is no truth as high as that of the Guru, there is no tapas higher than the Guru, there is no higher knowledge than His. Salutations to the Guru.

Mannāthaḥ śrī jagannāthaḥ/madguruḥ śrī jagadguruḥ
madātmā sarvabhūtātmā/tasmai śrī gurave namaḥ /12

My Lord is the Lord of the universe, my Guru is the Guru of the three worlds, my Self is the Self within all beings. Salutations to the Guru.

Gurur ādiranādiśca guruḥ/ paramadaivatam
guroḥ parataram nāsti/tasmai śrī gurave namaḥ /13

Though He lives, He was never born; the Satguru is the supreme truth. Above all else in the universe is the Satguru. Salutations to the Guru.

Devī Bhujaṅgam

Ṣaḍādhāra paṅkeruhāntar virājat
suṣumnāntarāleti tejollasantīm
vibantīm sudhāmaṇḍalam drāvayantīm
sudha mūrti mīḍhe mahānanta rūpām
/1

I bow before that personification of nectar, who is the ever lasting immortal bliss, who is the luster in the Sushumna, which is in the six chakras of the body, and who melts the moon and drinks its light.

Jvalat koṭi bālārka bhāsāruṇāṅgīm
sulāvaṇyaśṛṅgāra śobhābhirāmām
mahāpatma kiñjalkamadhye virājat
trikoṇollasantīm bhaje śrī bhavānīm /2

I sing about that Bhavani, who sits in the triangle, which shines in the stamen of the great lotus, who has the luster of crores of rising suns, who is immensely pretty, and who attracts the entire world by her charm.

Kvaṇal kiṅkiṇī nūvuro bhāsiranta prabhālīḍha lākṣārdra pādāravindam ajeśācyutādyais surais sevyamānām mahādevi! manmūrdhni te bhāvayāmi /3

O great goddess, please keep Your feet, which have jingling bells made of gems tied to it, which shine in the luster of Your wet lac painted feet, and which are worshipped by Vishnu, Brahma and others, on my head and bless me.

Suśoṇāmbarā badhnī virājan mahāratnakāñcīkalāpam nitambam sphuraddakṣiṇāvartanābhiścatisro valīramba! te romarājīm bhajeham /4

I worship the streak of hair on Your belly, Your shining navel circling to the left, Your hips dressed in red garments, and Your waist adorned with golden tinkling belt, studded with greatest of jewels.

Lasat vṛtta muttuṅga māṇikya kumbho
pama śrī stanadvantvam ambāmbujākṣi
bhaje dugdha pūrṇābhirāmam
tvadīyam
mahā hāra dīptam sadā vismitāsyam /5

I worship Your twin radiant raised breasts full of milk, which are round and like the gem studded pot, and which are ever shining with milk. Hey Mother who has lotus-like eyes.

Śirīṣa prasūnollasal bāhū daṇḍair
jjvalalbāṇakodaṇḍa pāśāmkuśāśca
calalkaṅkaṇoddāma keyūra bhūṣol
lasac chrīkarām bhojamābāhumīḍe /6

I worship that Bhavani, who glitters with her arms, which are as delicate as Sirisha flowers, and which carry arrow, bow, noose and goad, and which shine with bangles and bracelets.

Sunāsāpuṭam patma patrā yatākṣam
mukham devi bhakteṣ ṭada śrī kaṭākṣam
lalāṭ ojjvalat gandha kastūribhūṣ
ojjvalat pūrṇa candra prabham te
bhajeham /7

I worship that Bhavani, who is extremely pleasant, who shines like the full moon of autumn, whose lotus like face is adorned with peace, and who shines with a gem studded necklace and ear studs.

Calal kuntalānubhramal bhṛṅgavṛndair
ghanastigdha dhammila
bhūṣojjvalantīm
sphuran mauli māṇikya
baddhendurekhā
vilāsollasad divya murdhānamīḍe /8

I praise Your head, which is playfully radiant, which is adorned by the crescent moon, which is decorated by the line of gems, in whose dense hair the swarm of bees, enter, swirl and play, and which is decorated, by densely woven white jasmine flowers.

Iti śrī bhavānī svarūpam tavaivam
prapañcāl parañ cāti sūkṣmam
prasannam
sphuratvamba! ḍimbhasya me hṛt
saroje
sadā vāṅmayam sarva tejo maya tvam /9

This form of Yours, o Bhavani, which is much above the universe, in its micro form, may please shine in my lotus heart, and bless me in Your lustrous form, so that I rule over the wealth of words.

Gaṇeśāṇi mādyākhilaiś śakti vṛndaiḥ
Sphurat śrī mahā cakra rāje lasantīm
parām rājarājeśvarī traipurīm tvām
śivāṅkoparistham śivām tvam bhajeham
/10

I meditate on You, the wife of Shiva, who is sitting pleasantly on his lap, surrounded by Shaktis led by Lord Ganesha, who is sitting highly radiant on the chakra raja, and who is Tripura and Rajarajeshvari.

Tvam arkas tvam agnis tvam āpas tvam indus
tvam ākāśa bhūr vāyu sarvam tvameva
tvadanyam na kiṅcil prakāśosti sarvam
sadānanda saṁvitsvarūpam bhajeham /11

I sing about You in a form of blissful knowledge, as to whom there is none superior. You are sun, fire, water, and moon, You are ether, earth, and wind, You are everything indeed, You are the great essence.

Śivas tvam gurus tvaṇca śaktis tvameva
tvamevāsi mātā pita ca tvameva
tvamevāsi vidyā tvamevāsi bandhur
gatiramme matirdevi sarvam tvameva /12

You are lord Shiva, You are my teacher, You are the Goddess Shakti. You are my mother, You are my father, You are the knowledge, You are my relations, and so You are my only refuge, my only thought. Everything that I can think of is You.

**Śrutī nāmagamyam purāṇairagamyam
mahimnānu jānanti pāram tavātra
stutim kartumicchāmi te tvam bhavāni
kṣamasvaivam amba pramugdhaḥ
kilāham /13**

Though I don't know Your greatness, wish I to praise You, o Bhavani. You are the knower of Vedas and Agamas, and You are unreachable through scriptures. So please pardon me for doing this.

**Śaraṇyai vareṇyai sukāruṇya pūrṇair
hiraṇyodarādyai ragaṇyais supūrṇaiḥ
bhavāraṇya bhītaśca mām pāhi bhadre
namaste namaste punaste namostu! /14**

Salutations, salutations, and salutations, o Bhavani. You are my refuge, my boon and form of all mercy, You are greatest among all devas, o holy one, and so, please protect me from this forest snare of life.

Bhavānī bhavānī bhavānīti vaṇī
mudārāmudāram mudā ye bhajanti
na śoko na pāpo na rogo na mṛtyuḥ
kadācil kadacil kadacinnarāṇām /15

Three times repeat the holy name of Bhavani, with devotion and repeatedly for ever, and get rid of sorrow, passion, sin and fear, for all time and for all ways.

Idam śuddhacitto bhavānī bhujaṅgam
paṭhan buddhimān bhaktiyuktaśca tasmai
svakīyam padam śāśvatam vedasāram
śriyaṅceṣṭasiddhiśca devīdadāti /16

Who ever correctly reads with devotion, this great hymn praising Bhavani from head to toe, would attain a permanent place of salvation, which is the essence of Vedas, and also get wealth and the eight occult powers.

Annapūrṇa Stotram

Hymn to the All-Nourishing Mother

Nityānandakarī varābhayakarī
saundaryaratnākarī
nirdhūtākhila ghora pāpanikarī
pratyakṣa māheśvarī
prāleyācala vamśa pāvanakarī
kāśīpuraādhīśvarī
bhikṣām dehi kṛpāvalambanakarī
mātānnapūrṇeśvarī /1

O Mother Annapūrneshvari, please bestow alms upon me. You dispense eternal happiness as well as boons and protection. Our fears are dispelled by You. By washing away our sins You grant us mental purity. O great goddess, You purified the race of Himavan. Ruler of Kashi, You are the embodiment of mercy.

Nānāratna vicitrabhūṣaṇakarī
hemāmbarāḍambarī
mūktāhāra vilambamāna
vilasadvakṣojakumbhāntarī

kāṣmīrā garuvāsitā rucikarī
kāśīpurādhīśvarī
bhikṣām dehi kṛpāvalambanakarī
mātānnapūrṇeśvarī /2

O Mother Annapūrneshvari, please bestow alms upon me. Your hands are adorned with ornaments and jewels and You are beautifully clothed in golden attire. Upon Your breasts and waist rest garlands made of pearl. You are wonderfully fragrant with the frankincense of Kashmir, O incarnation of beauty. Ruler of Kashi, You are the embodiment of mercy.

Yogānandakarī ripukṣayakarī
dharmaikaniṣṭhākarī
candrārkānalabhāsamānalaharī
trailokyarakṣākarī
sarvaiśvarya karī tapaḥ phalakarī
kāśīpurādhīśvarī
bhikṣām dehi kṛpāvalambanakarī
mātānnapūrṇeśvarī /3

O Mother Annapūrneshvari, please bestow alms upon me. You dispense the bliss of Yoga. By Your grace our enemies are destroyed and our feet are set firmly on the path of dharma. You display the radiance of the moon, the sun and fire. The three worlds are protected by You. All prosperity and all of the rewards for penance flow from You. Ruler of Kashi, You are the embodiment of mercy.

Kailāsācala kandarālayakarī gaurī umā
śaṅkarī
kaumārī nigamārthagocarakarī
omkārabījākṣarī
mokṣadvārakavāṭapāṭanakarī
kāśīpurādhīśvarī
bhikṣām dehi kṛpāvalambanakarī
mātānnapūrṇeśvarī /4

O Mother Annapūrneshvari, please bestow alms upon me. You dwell amidst the caves of Mount Kailash. O Uma, You radiate a golden hue. Consort of Lord Shiva, blessed with eternal youth, You reveal the inner meaning of the

Vedas. Embodiment of 'OM,' You open the door to eternal liberation. Ruler of Kashi, You are the embodiment of mercy.

Dṛśyādṛśya vibhūtivāhanakarī
brahmāṇḍabhāṇḍodarī
līlānāṭaka sūtra bhedanakarī
vijñānadīpāṅkurī
śrī viśveśāmanaḥ prasādakarī
kāśīpurādhīśvarī
bhikṣām dehi kṛpāvalambanakarī
mātānnapūrṇeśvarī /5

O Mother Annapūrneshvari, please bestow alms upon me. You grant all visible and invisible blessings. The entire universe is contained in You. This world is a drama that You have staged. You are the fire in the torch of wisdom. The mind of the Lord of the universe is pleased by You. Ruler of Kashi, You are the embodiment of mercy.

Urvīsarvajaneśvarī jayakarī
mātākṛpāsāgarī
veṇīnīlasamānakuntaladharī
nityānnadāneśvarī
sākṣānmokṣakarī sadā śubhakarī
kāśīpurādhīśvarī
bhikṣām dehi kṛpāvalambanakarī
mātānnapūrṇeśvarī /6

O Mother Annapūrneshvari, please bestow alms upon me. You are the queen of the world. Showering Your motherly love on all, You insure success. O ocean of kindness, with locks of beautiful hair arranged in braids, You provide the means of sustenance to all beings. Granting salvation to all, Your every action is auspicious. Ruler of Kashi, You are the embodiment of mercy.

Ādikṣānta samasta varṇanakari
śambhostri bhāvākarī
kāśmīrā tripureśvarī triṇayanī
viśveśvarī śarvarī
kāmākāṅkṣakarī janodayakarī
kāśīpurādhīśvarī

**bhikṣām dehi kṛpāvalambanakarī
mātānnapūrṇeśvarī /7**

O Mother Annapūrneshvari, please bestow alms upon me. The letters of the alphabet were first invented by You. You monitor Shambu's three-fold aspect of creation, protection and destruction. Covered in saffron, partner of the three-eyed destroyer of Tripura, ruler of the universe, You perfect in Yourself the beauty of the night and You open wide the doors to heaven. Ruler of Kashi, You are the embodiment of mercy.

**Devī sarva vicitraratnaracitā dākṣāyaṇī
sundarī
vāmā svādupayodharā priyakarī
saubhāgya māheśvarī
bhaktābhīṣṭakarī sadā śubhakarī
kāśīpurādhīśvarī
bhikṣām dehi kṛpāvalambanakarī
mātānnapūrṇeśvarī /8**

O Mother Annapūrneshvari, please bestow alms upon me. O radiant one, adorned with a display of rare jewels, charming daughter of Daksha,

You are blessed with perfect manners and noble virtues. Always engaged in auspicious acts, You grant the desires of those who earnestly open their hearts to You. Ruler of Kashi, You are the embodiment of mercy.

Candrārkānalakoṭi koṭisadṛśī candrām
śubimbādharī
candrārkāgni samāna kuṇḍaladharī
candrārkavarṇeśvarī
mālāpustakapāśasāṅkuśadharī
kāśīpurādhīśvarī
bhikṣām dehi kṛpāvalambanakarī
mātānnapūrṇeśvarī /9

O Mother Annapūrneshvari, please bestow alms upon me. The splendor of Your form is greater even than that of thousands of moons, suns and fires combined together. Your lips resemble rare and luscious fruit and are as pleasant as moonlight. In beauty You surpass the celestial orbs. In Your hands You clasp a garland, a book, a rope and a goad. Ruler of Kashi, You are the embodiment of mercy.

Kṣatratrāṇakarī mahābhayakarī mātā kṛpāsāgarī
sarvānandakarī sadā śivakarī viśveśvarīśrīdharī
dakṣākrandakarī nirāmayakarī kāśīpurādhīśvarī
bhikṣām dehi kṛpāvalambanakarī mātānnapūrṇeśvarī /10

O Mother Annapūrneshvari, please bestow alms upon me. You grant protection like a warrior and thus dispel all fears. O mother, ocean of kindness, You provide all with happiness. Auspicious one, You hold sway over this universe and control destiny. You brought great distress to Daksha Prajapati. All ailments are cured by You. Ruler of Kashi, You are the embodiment of mercy.

Annapūrṇe sadāpūrṇe śaṅkaraprāṇavallabhe
jñānavairāgya siddhyartham bhikṣām dehi ca pārvati /11

O Annapoorna, You are ever full. Radiating the essence of life, never exhausted, O partner of Shankara, grant to me that I become fully established in knowledge and renunciation.

Mātā me pārvatī devi pitā devo
maheśvaraḥ
bāndhavāḥ śivabhaktāśca svadeśo
bhuvanatrayam /12

Parvati Devi is my Divine Mother and Lord Mahesvara is my Father. My family encompasses the devotees of Shiva; all the three worlds are my native lands.

Bhagavad Gītā – Chapter 8

Chanted in Amritapuri on special occasions such as funeral rites

Athāṣṭo'dhyāyaḥ akṣarabrahma yogaḥ
Eighth chapter, 'The Yoga of the Imperishable Brahman'

Arjuna uvāca
Arjuna said:

Kim tad brahma kim adhyātmam/kim karma puruṣottama
adhibhūtam ca kim proktam/ adhidaivam kim ucyate /1

What is that Brahman? What is the Adhyatma (the essential Self)? What is action? O best among men, what is declared to be the Abhibhoota (the Lord of beings)? And what is Adhidaiva (Lord of Gods) said to be?

Adhiyajñaḥ katham ko'tra/dehe'smin madhusūdana
prayāṇakāle ca katham/jñeyo'si niyatātmabhiḥ /2

When and how is Adhiyajna here in this body, O destroyer of Madhu? And how, at the time of death, are You to be known by the self controlled?

Śrī Bhagavān uvāca

The Blessed Lord said:

Akṣaram brahma paramam/ svabhāvo'dhyātmam ucyate
bhūta bhāvod bhava karo/visargaḥ karma saṁjñitaḥ /3

Brahman is the Imperishable, the Supreme, His essential nature is called Self knowledge. The creative force that causes beings to spring forth into manifestation is called work.

Adhibhūtam kṣaro bhāvaḥ/puruṣaś cādhidaivatam
adhiyajño'ham evātra/dehe dehabhṛtām vara /4

Adhiboota constitutes My perishable nature and the Indweller is the Adhidaivata. I alone am the Adhiyajna here in this body, O Arjuna.

Antakāle ca māmeva/smaran muktvā kalevaram
yaḥ prayāti sa madbhāvam/yāti nāstyatra saṁśayaḥ /5

And whosoever leaving the body goes forth remembering Me alone, at the time of death he attains My being. There is no doubt about this.

Yam yam vāpi smaran bhāvam/ tyajatyante kalevaram
tam tam evaiti kaunteya/sadā tadbhāvabhāvitaḥ /6

Whosoever, upon leaving the body, he goes to whatever being he dwells upon. This is because of his constant thought upon that being.

Tasmāt sarveṣu kāleṣu/mām anusmara yudhya ca
mayy arpita mano buddhir/mām evaiṣyasy asaṁśayaḥ /7

Therefore, at all times, remember Me and fight. With mind and intellect fixed on Me, you shall doubtless come to Me alone.

Abhyāsa yoga yuktena/cetasā nānya gāminā
paramam puruṣam divyam/yāti pārthānucintayan /8

One who withdraws the mind from all distractions, holds it steadfast through the method of habitual meditation and constantly meditates on the Supreme Purusha, the Resplendent, such a person goes to the Supreme.

Kavim purāṇam anuśāsitāram aṇor aṇīyāṁsam anusmared yaḥ
sarvasya dhātāram acintya rūpam āditya varṇam tamasaḥ parastāt /9

Whosoever meditates upon the Omniscient, the Ancient, the Ruler, That which is more minute than an atom, the Supporter of all, of inconceivable form, effulgent like the sun and beyond darkness.

Prayāṇa kāle manasācalena bhaktyā
yukto yoga balena caiva
bhruvor madhye prāṇam āveśya
saṁyak sa tam param puruṣam
upaiti divyam /10

At the time of death, with an unshaken mind full of devotion, fixing the life energy between the eyebrows with the power of yoga, such a one reaches the resplendent, supreme Purusha

Yad akṣaram vedavido vadanti/ viśanti
yad yatayo vītarāgāḥ
yad icchanto brahmacaryam caranti/
tat te padam saṅgraheṇa pravakṣye
/11

That which is declared Imperishable by those knowledgeable in the Veda, that which the self controlled and those free of desire enter, that desiring which Brahmacharya is practised, that goal I will declare to you in brief.

Sarva dvārāṇi saṁyamya/mano hṛdi nirudhya ca
mūrdhny ādhāyātmanaḥ prāṇam/ āsthito yogadhāraṇām /12

Controlling all of the senses, having confined the mind in the heart, centering the life energy within, engaged in the practice of concentration.

Om ity ekākṣaram brahma/vyāharan mām anusmaran
yaḥ prayāti tyajan deham/sa yāti paramām gatim /13

Uttering the one syllabled 'Om', the symbol of Brahman, and remembering Me, such a one attains the Supreme goal when departing from the body.

Ananya cetāḥ satatam yo/mām smarati nityaśaḥ
tasyāham sulabhaḥ pārtha/nitya yuktasya yoginaḥ /14

I am easily attainable by that Yogi, ever-steadfast, who constantly remembers Me, every day, without thinking of anything else, O Arjuna.

Mām upetya punar janma/duḥkhālayam aśāśvatam
nāpnuvanti mahātmānaḥ/saṁsiddhim paramām gatāḥ /15

Having attained Me, these great souls do not take birth again in this ephemeral abode of pain. They attain the highest perfection.

Ābrahma bhuvanāl lokāḥ/punar āvartino'rjuna
mām upetya tu kaunteya/punar janma na vidyate /16

All the worlds up to and including that of Brahma, the creator, are subject to rebirth, O Arjuna. But he who reaches Me is never reborn.

Sahasra yuga paryantam/ahar yad brahmaṇo viduḥ
rātrim yuga sahasrāntām/te'ho rātra vido janāḥ /17

Those who know the length of the Day of Brahma and the Night of Brahma, which each lasts for a thousand eons, they know day and night.

Avyaktād vyaktayaḥ sarvāḥ/ prabhavanty aharāgame
rātry āgame pralīyante/tatraivāvyakta sāṁjñake /18

From the unmanifested all the manifested proceed at the coming of the Day. At the coming of Night they dissolve into that same unmanifested.

Bhūta grāmaḥ sa evāyam/bhūtvā bhūtvā pralīyate
rātry āgame'vaśaḥ pārtha/prabhavaty ahar āgame /19

The multitude of beings are helplessly bom and dissolved again and again, O Arjuna, during the successive days and nights of Brahma.

Paras tasmāt tu bhāvo'nyo/'vyakto'vyaktāt sanātanaḥ
yaḥ sa sarveṣu bhūteṣu/naśyatsu na vinaśyati /20

But verily there is the eternal existence beyond the unmanifest. It is not destroyed when all beings are destroyed.

Avyakto'kṣara ity uktas/tam āhuḥ paramām gatim
yam prāpya na nivartante/tad dhāma paramam mama /21

This Imperishable is the highest goal. They who reach it never return. That is My highest abode.

Puruṣaḥ sa paraḥ pārtha/bhaktyā labhyas tvananyayā
yasyāntaḥ sthāni bhūtāni/yena sarvam idam tatam /22

That highest Purusha, O Arjuna, is attainable through unswerving devotion to It. In That all beings dwell, by That all this is pervaded.

Yatra kāle tvanāvṛttim/āvṛttim caiva yoginaḥ
prayātā yānti tam kālam/vakṣyāmi bharatarṣabha /23

Now I will tell you at what time Yogins depart only to return again, and at what time Yogins depart never to return again.

Agnir jyotir ahaḥ śuklaḥ/ṣaṇmāsā uttarāyaṇam
tatra prayātā gacchanti/brahma brahma vido janāḥ /24

Fire, light, day-time, the bright fortnight and the six months of the northern solstice, following this path those who know Brahman go to Brahman.

Dhūmo rātris tathā kṛṣṇaḥ/ṣaṇmāsā dakṣiṇāyanam
tatra cāndramasam jyotir/yogī prāpya nivartate /25

Smoke, night time, the dark fortnight and the six months of the summer solstice, following this path and attaining the lunar light, the Yogin returns.

Śuklakṛṣṇe gatī hyete/jagataḥ śāśvate mate

ekayā yāty anāvṛttim/anyayā'vartate punaḥ /26

The path of light and the path of darkness, both available to the world, are eternal. By the path of light, a man goes and does not return; from the path of darkness he returns again.

Naite sṛtī pārtha jānan/yogī muhyati kaścana
tasmāt sarveṣu kāleṣu/yogayukto bhavārjuna /27

Knowing these paths, O Arjuna, no Yogin is deluded. Therefore, at all times be steadfast in Yoga.

Vadeṣu yajñeṣu tapaḥsu caiva dāneṣu yat puṇya phalam pradiṣṭam
atyeti tat sarvam idam viditvā yogī param sthānam upaiti cādyam /28

Whatever merit one attains through study of the Vedas, from the performance of sacrifices or from the practice of austerities and charity, beyond the attainment of this merit goes the Yogin who, having known these two paths, attains to the Supreme.

Om tat sat iti śrīmad bhagavadgītāsu upaniṣadsu brahma vidyāyām
yoga śāstre śrī kṛṣṇārjuna saṁvāde
akṣarabrahma yogo nāmāṣṭo'dhyāyaḥ

Thus, in the Upanishad sung by the Lord, the science of Brahman, the scripture of Yoga, the dialogue between Sri Krishna and Arjuna, ends the eighth chapter, entitled 'The Yoga of the Imperishable Brahman'

Om sarva dharmān parityajya mām
ekam śaraṇam vraja
aham tvā sarva pāpebhyo mokṣayiṣyāmi
mā śucaḥ (Ch. 18.66)

Relinquishing all dharmas take refuge in Me alone. I will liberate you from all sins; do not grieve.

Amma's Websites

AMRITAPURI—Amma's Home Page
Teachings, Activities, Ashram Life, eServices, Yatra, Blogs and News
http://www.amritapuri.org

AMMA USA
About Amma, Meeting Amma, Global Charities, Groups and Activities and Teachings
http://www.amma.org

EMBRACING THE WORLD®
Basic Needs, Emergencies, Environment, Research and News
http://www.embracingtheworld.org

AMRITA UNIVERSITY
About, Admissions, Campuses, Academics, Research, Global and News
http://www.amrita.edu

THE AMMA SHOP—Embracing the World® Books & Gifts Shop
Blog, Books, Complete Body, Home & Gifts, Jewelry, Music and Worship
http://www.theammashop.org

IAM—Integrated Amrita Meditation Technique®
Meditation Taught Free of Charge to the Public, Students, Prisoners and Military
http://www.amma.org/groups/north-america/projects/iam-meditation-classes

AMRITA PUJA
Types and Benefits of Pujas, Brahmasthanam Temple, Astrology Readings, Ordering Pujas
http://www.amritapuja.org

GREENFRIENDS
Growing Plants, Building Sustainable Environments, Education and Community Building
http://www.amma.org/groups/north-america/projects/green-friends

FACEBOOK
This is the Official Facebook Page to Connect with Amma
https://www.facebook.com/MataAmritanandamayi

DONATION PAGE
Please Help Support Amma's Charities Here:
http://www.amma.org/donations

AMMA EUROPE
www.amma-europe.org

www.ingramcontent.com/pod-product-compliance
Lightning Source LLC
Chambersburg PA
CBHW061338040426
42444CB00011B/2988
9781680370584